v TO

RT A

IPATIVE

EMENT

PROGRAM

How To
Start A
Participative
Management
Program

10 Easy Steps

By
Jerre G. Lewis
Leslie D. Renn

Lewis & Renn Associates, Inc.
Interlochen, Michigan

*Additional copies of this book may be ordered through bookstores
or by sending $9.95 plus $2.50 for postage and handling to
Publishers Distribution Service
121 E. Front Street, Suite 203
Traverse City, MI 49684
1-800-345-0096*

Publisher's Cataloging-in-Publication Data

Lewis, Jerre G., 1937-
    How to start a participative management program :
    ten key steps / by Jerre G. Lewis and Leslie D. Renn--
    Interlochen, MI : Lewis & Renn Associates.
       p.   cm.
    Includes bibliography and index.
    ISBN 0-9628759-1-0
  1. Management--Employee participation. 2. Decision-making, group.
  3. Quality of work life. I. Renn, Leslie, D., 1940-
  II. Title

HD5650.L49   1992
658.3'--dc20   91-90576

Manufactured in the United States of America

To my wife Victoria, and my children Elizabeth, Marie, John, and Becky Lewis.

To my wife Donna, and my children Leslie, Kevin, Jeffrey, and Christine Renn.

Preface

How To Start A Participative Management Program is for those businessmen and women who are interested in improving their organizational productivity and the quality of working life for their employees. It provides the 10 necessary steps for implementing a successful participative management and employee involvement program. The book is written in such a way that the material can be grasped by business practitioners having little or no background on the subject. This book presents a step-by-step approach to empowering employees and giving them the opportunity to become involved in the decision making process relative to their own jobs. For many years, traditional management prevailed in the United States, and employees were treated as economic beings. Managers hired employees to do a specific job, and rewarded them with a weekly paycheck to satisfy their physiological needs. Today, employees want more than just their paycheck. They want to be challenged on their jobs—They want to self-actualize using their full potential on the job. They want their needs met on the job. Managers can no longer overlook these needs and continue to operate their businesses efficiently. Employee involvement and participative management programs have been promoted enthusiastically in recent years, and many feel it is the only way to regain America's competitive edge. This book tells the reader how to get started in implementing such a program. Participative management is a whole new way of managing a business. It means trusting employees, involving employees in the business, asking employees for their opinions and recommendations on issues affecting their jobs, and in many cases changing from an adversarial work climate to one of a high quality of working life where employees enjoy coming to work and becoming involved. Any businessperson contemplating a move to a more participative style of managing their business must read this book. It tells the reader how to do it in an effective manner.

Contents

How To
Start A
Participative
Management
Program

Chapter 1

Introduction

Participative management is defined broadly as a manager sharing decision making with subordinates. This concept has been promoted enthusiastically in recent years and many who write and talk about the subject insist that it is essential for regaining America's competitive edge in the world market (Herman, 1989). Participation is most useful in problem solving and direction setting. It is a tool for managers looking for creativity and synergy. Its value is in its power to accomplish business objectives (Uzzi, 1989).

An effective participative management program is one that has mutual individual employee participation and cooperation in decision-making, responsive to the problems and needs of the organization. Real employee involvement will be voluntary, self-motivating, and intrinsic in nature. This positive involvement will improve the processes of the organization and ultimately organizational effectiveness. Some indicators of an effective participative management program are improved trust and individual commitment, support of top management and the local union, increased communication, training and motivation, improved management of conflict, more effective problem solving, and more flexible forms of work and work organization.

The impact of employee involvement and productivity suggest that the more intense employee involvement and joint labor-management efforts are, the more likely they are to positively affect performance (Cooke, 1986). This value-based process is aimed toward meeting the twin goals of enhanced effectiveness of the firm and improved quality of life at work for employees (Fulmer and Coleman, 1984).

Chapter 2

Background

Participative management and employee involvement is a process by which an organization attempts to unlock the creative potential of its people by involving them in decisions affecting their work lives. A distinguishing characteristic of the process is that its goals are not simply extrinsic, focusing on the improvement of productivity and efficiency per se, but they are also intrinsic regarding what the worker sees as self-fulfilling and self-enhancing ends in themselves (Guest, R. 1979).

As a practical matter, participative management, employee involvement, and quality of work life represents a major shift in management style. The traditional adversarial relationship between management and labor is eschewed in favor of cooperation as employee involvement is based on the assumption that organizational goals and personal goals are fundamentally not in conflict and that each set of goals can be accomplished to the benefit of all concerned (Fulmer, &

Coleman, 1984). Because one of the key goals of employee involvement programs is to enhance the quality of the employees' working life, management must be responsive to the desires of the employees. The best way to ascertain those desires is to ask employees. "While sociologists, psychologists, and human relations specialists may make suggestions on how assembly lines could be made more humane and less boring, the workers probably know best what it will take to make them happier, more contented, and, most important perhaps, more productive" says John Runcie (1980, p.111). Thus, it is easily understood that: "A style of management that invites participation or consultation from members of the workforce on matters that affect them, and with regard to which they might have some pertinent ideas is an essential condition for an employee involvement and quality of work life program" says Edward Glazer (1976, p.39-40).

A number of companies and unions have been experimenting with new strategies for improving the performance of their bargaining relationships at the plant level through what generally have been labeled employee involvement and quality of work life programs. The now famous QWL experiment at GM's beleaguered Tarrytown, N.Y., plant is a classic example of employee involvement as union-management collaboration. Born of frustration and despair, the project that began in 1971 "involved a mutual commitment by management and the union to change old ways of dealing with work on the shop floor" says Dale Feuer (1989, p.39-40).

While participation in the workplace has been tried as a solution to a multitude of organizational problems, with varying degrees of effectiveness, two goals emerge as common to all employee involvement programs. One is to improve working conditions in some way for employees, whether as a means to an end in itself. The other is to increase employee involvement in problem solving and/or decision making (Feuer, 1989).

A notable increase in communication among various groups at Illinois Bell has come about through union and management participation in an employee involvement and quality of work life project. Some productivity improvements have been achieved, but are not stressed, according to Irv Kamradt, the firm's QWL director. Illinois Bell's way of addressing work life issues is through a committee of managers and union representatives. Employee involvement is achieved by indirection rather than through organized groups in the work units. This arrangement has led to greater trust among managers and union representatives and has opened communication (Farish, 1986).

When the old General Motors Plant in Fremont, California began turning out cars again, the only carryovers from the old system were the shell of the old main building and some of the former employees. Just about everything else was new such as corporate sponsorship, operating philosophy, and the manufacturing system. The New United Motor Manufacturing, Inc. is a joint venture of General Motors and Toyota. It was set up as a means through which General Motors could learn the Japanese Manufacturing system, and the Japanese could learn how to operate in an American context (Farish, 1986). An open environment was established at Nummi in which joint problem solving by labor and management, seeking options for mutual gain while developing good faith and trust prevailed.

"The quality of life at work in turn results in better performance and higher productivity on the job" says Theodore Mills, director of the American Quality of Work Center. He reports that he does not know of a single instance where improved quality of working life didn't lead to improved productivity (1978, p.10).

If workers can be motivated and given the opportunity to participate in the search for improved methods of job performance, and if this motivation and participation can be maintained over time, job performance should improve (Vroom, V. 1964).

Productivity is higher in enterprises with an organized program of worker participation. Employee participation, if done right, can and does raise productivity. The most appropriate form will no doubt vary from company to company but participation, like marriage, works only when both parties want it to work. The solution to America's pathetic productivity growth isn't necessarily more capital spending. Several studies show that giving workers more responsibility can have a marked effect (Blinder, 1989).

Cooperation can be sustained if labor and management submit to certain conditions. There must be mutual respect, acceptance by management of the union's legitimacy in those organizations where unions are present, a reasonable guarantee that participation will not cause layoffs or otherwise hurt workers, and an understanding that the benefits derived from participation will be shared equitably between the needs of the employer and those of the employee (St.Cyr, 1984).

People tend to accomplish what they decide they want to accomplish. Ideas, changes, suggestions and recommendations that are generated by the people who must implement them stand a much greater chance of being successfully implemented (Uzzi, 1989). In theory, people who have a hand in making a decision are better motivated to execute it. Participation can improve the quality of decision making especially since many of those extra heads are close to the action (Herman, 1989).

When jobs are challenging, workers are committed and perform superbly. What has been a slow evolution of employee involvement is turning into a revolution in the way work is organized and managed in the United States companies that only a few years ago disdained participation are rushing to set up so-called self-managing work teams, the most advanced stage of employee involvement. The team concept is spreading rapidly in industries such as autos, aerospace, electrical equipment, electronics, food processing, paper, steel, and even financial services. Although work teams differ from company to company, they typically consist of 5 to 12 multi-skilled workers who rotate jobs and produce an entire product or service with only minimal supervision. Adopting the team approach is no small matter; it means wiping out tiers of managers and tearing down bureaucratic barriers between departments. Yet companies are willing to undertake such radical changes to gain workers' knowledge and commitment along with productivity gains that exceed 30 percent in some cases (Hoerr, 1989).

The actual process of involvement in a participative process both increases the interest of participants in the process and broadens their notion of the content areas over which they should have influence (Spector, 1986).

Chapter 3

10 Steps To Implementing A Successful
Participative Management Program

Step #1

Support of top management and union leadership. Top management must sanction and be supportive of any participative management and employee involvement program. A noticeable shift in the distribution of decision making power and authority will occur within the management ranks as employees become involved in decision making. Management must be fully convinced and committed to such a program before embarking on this journey. It is very important that once top management has made the decision in favor of participative management, all supervisory personnel be properly trained on how to change their management style from the old traditional hardline approach to the participatory style. It is one thing for management to tell their supervisors that they are going to start managing in a participatory manner, but it is another thing to show them how to do it. This comes with proper training and coaching. It is very unfortunate when supervisors are willing to change but don't know how to go about doing it. Without proper education and training of supervisory personnel and support of top management, failure will be the result of an employee involvement program.

Union leadership must also be prepared for embarking on a participative management program. Many union leaders have feared that participative management and employee involvement programs would undermine the role of the local union and the collective bargaining agreements. It must be remembered and realized that participative management programs and collective bargaining agreements are two separate issues and must be handled as such. Union leaders must be prepared to continue to represent their rank and file in the same manner as previously, even with the emergence of an employee involvement program. Union leadership must be ready to embark on such a program of employee involvement and be supportive of top management as such. Without the support of the union leadership, the program will fail.

Step #2

The employees must be ready to accept a participative management program, which means all employees, management, clerical, and hourly. In order for employees to be receptive to such a program, a culture change must occur. Implementing a participative management program in an adversarial work climate will not work and be successful. Employees must be willing to change and desire to start working together as a team. This culture change does not happen overnight. It must be a way of life or commonly called the quality of work life. Management must initiate this culture change through the way it manages and involves its employees. Everyone in the organization must have the same equal opportunity to become involved in decision making relative to their own job. In other words, the hourly workforce cannot be given the opportunity to participate at the expense of the salary employees.

Step #3

Establish trust amongst all employees. Trust is the glue that binds employees together in an organization. An employee involvement program will not be a success without trust. Management must initiate trust among its employees. Trust is not purchased. It is earned. In order for trust to occur, honesty and integrity must prevail. Management should not make any promises to its employees that it can not deliver on and back up. An example would be management telling its employees that if they become involved in a participative management program and come up with some cost savings ideas and job improvements, their jobs would be secure and then when a downturn in sales occurs, employees would be laid off. This occurrence would destroy any trust that was initiated between the employees and management. If such a promise was made on job security, then these employees should be retrained and assigned to another position in the organization. Trust is an extremely important element in any participative management program and must be established as such or the program will not be a success. Employees must be able to trust one another and support each other.

Step #4

Any participative management and employee involvement program should be initiated on a voluntary basis. Employees should not be forced to participate in decision making against their own will. The results would be disastrous. Not everyone is born to be a decision maker. Once an employee decides not to become involved in such a program, he should not be pegged as refusing to be a team player and viewed in a negative manner. It is very important that the attitudes of these employees continue to be respected.

Step #5

A participative management program should not be implemented "wholesale" across the entire organization. It should start in small departmental groups where there is a consensus that the employees are willing to get together to discuss mutual problems and come up with some solutions. It is very important that once ideas come forward from the groups, management should be ready to follow up and implement these ideas whenever feasible. It is advisable to start with the easier problems first and then go to the more difficult problems later.

Step # 6

Management should not initiate a participative management program to try to save an organization from destruction as a last chance effort. An employee involvement program should not be used as an alternative when other more serious changes need to be made first in an organization. These programs have been used in organizations for the above reasons and have failed because of their intent and because they were implemented too late.

Step # 7

Participative management and employee involvement programs must be results oriented.

If management is going to ask employees for their input and suggestions relative to their own job, it is very important that they follow up and provide the necessary resources to make the program work. It will not work with lip service. The program must produce some results such as cost savings or it will lose its credibility and ultimately fail. Goals and objectives must be set and employees must know what is expected of them. They can not be left alone to do their own thing. There must be adequate control measures in place at all times. It is also important that the program be continually evaluated for its effectiveness.

Step # 8

Employees must be given the proper training in problem solving, planning, financial analysis, and communication techniques in order to participative effectively in an employee involvement program. Management must be willing to open the books of the organization to employees and communicate financial information to them to assist them on their projects.

Step # 9

Any participative management program involves risk taking on the part of management. Employee involvement means management must share decision making but not responsibility. Managers must manage the business and keep control of the organization. Management is the risk taker and is at risk in any participative management program. Risk taking is absolutely essential in any employee involvement program.

Step # 10

Employees can become involved in many different stages of the decision making process meaning that they are not necessarily always required to make only final decisions. What is important is that the employees are clear about what is expected of them in their involvement in the participative management program. It is important to remember that participation and employee involvement can improve the overall quality of the decisions being made because the employees are closer to the problems on their jobs. Asking employees questions about issues on their jobs is very beneficial as they are the most knowledgeable. Employees must develop a sense of ownership in the business and have a positive impact on the business and the bottom line. Employees must understand the business such as costs, profits, waste, and value-added to enable them to translate this knowledge into a personal competitive advantage on the job. They must also know their competition and how they stack up against it. It is important that employees understand what it takes to be successful such as high quality, low cost and on-time delivery (Moskal, 1988).

Chapter 4

A Move To Participative Management

A complete move to a participatory style of management, company-wide , takes time. Companies must pass through various evolutionary states. This usually begins with some formal participatory structure. Programs such as employee participation groups, self-managed groups, shared-management groups, quality circles, and other worker involvement teams are often helpful. A network of work effectiveness teams is usually the first experience of participatory management in many companies. But the full fruit of participatory management is borne when the company abandons the formal structure and continues to work participatively (Uzzi, 1989).

Employee participation group programs are usually formed around the desire of some employees to have some impact on their respective jobs and how they are accomplished. These groups normally are formed within a department with a leader usually appointed by the group. The group leaders also meet monthly with the joint union-management leadership group. Some of the employee participation groups may ask for more responsibility and authority and may then evolve into self-managed or shared-management groups. Self-managed groups set their own goals, map their schedules, handle absenteeism, set production, quality and delivery targets, and even sign their own timecards without a boss. Shared-management groups do the same, but include a supervisor or manager in their group to act as a helper or coach when the group itself can't accomplish an objective. Under this approach, supervisors can coach several groups (Moskal, 1988).

In Japan, group autonomy is encouraged by avoiding any reliance on experts to solve operational problems. One widely used group-based technique for dealing with such problems is quality control (QC) circles. A QC circle's major task is to pinpoint and solve a particular workshop's problem. Outside experts are called in only to educate group members in the analytical tools for problem-solving or to provide a specialized technical service (Tubbs, 1988).

Usually in a participatory environment, the management philosophy is to empower employees and push decision making down to the lowest level so that ideas for empowerment can originate either with the employees or from within the ranks of management.

Some organizations involved in participative management are jointly operated by management and the union. Decisions are made jointly. Problems are solved jointly. Management staff meetings are expanded to include union leaders. This ensures union involvement in the organization's decision-making forum. The joint staff meets weekly. Management doesn't act unilaterally. Decisions are made by consensus (Moskal, 1988).

In order to help change management's ideas about labor, and labor's ideas about management, and to sometimes overcome initial resistance to a joint business operation, promoting the formation of several joint committees to address common organizational problems is a good idea. These committees can be the first small steps in doing business together. Many business organizations realize that things have to be done differently if they are going to survive in the marketplace. In many cases, they are not making it with the old system of operating. Sharing information like market share and sales with employees, and helping them to understand that jobs and profitability go hand in hand is important. Once the magnitude of a problem is understood, employees attention becomes engaged, and as they receive the needed knowledge about their place of business, the appeal for solutions is given to them (Moskal, 1988).

Before an organization moves to a participatory style of managing, it is very important to survey the employees to find out their feelings about employee involvement, and where the organization is as far as the people element is concerned. Refer to Appendix A for a Pre-Employee Participative Management Survey which should be administered before any employee involvement program is ever implemented. After a Participative Management Program has been implemented for at least one year, A Post Employee Participative Management Survey should be administered to find out the employees perception of the program. Refer to Appendix B for the survey.

Chapter 5

Implementing The Participative Management Process

Why would a manager want to implement a participative management and employee involvement program? The reasons are many. One reason may be due to the lack of profitability of the business organization. Decline in sales, profit margin, return on sales, and reduced productivity may be all involved. Management may have decided to finally turn to its employees and involve them in decision making to help the organization turn around profitability wise. Management may have decided that their present style of managing did not work and they needed to change and involve their employees to get the business proceeding in the proper direction. Another reason for managers to turn to participative management may be as a last chance effort to save the business from failure and bankruptcy. The business will not survive unless a management change is implemented. Involving the employees in decision making to save the business may be the manager's goal. A

manager may turn to participative management
to create better relationships between the union
and management and between the employees
and management. Some organizations have
operated very successfully on a financial basis
but turned to employee involvement because
management wanted to have a close harmonious
relationship with the employees and develop a
team approach. By doing this, there will be much
less arguing and grievances filed, thus eliminat-
ing the adversarial climate which really in all
practicality is a waste of time. When employee
grievances are being filed, what this indicates is
that the problems could not be resolved between
the employees and management. Implementing
employee involvement programs helps to elimi-
nate these kinds of problems. In some organizations, there have been some instances where
some members of management and union officials failed to communicate for some fifteen years.
A manager may want a participative management program started to get employees together
to begin communicating with each other rather
than hating each other and considering each
other an enemy. Union officials hope to gain a
better working environment for their rank and
file by becoming involved in these programs, and
also to receive increased job security for its
members. Union officials take a risk when

becoming involved in these programs as they may be accused of not representing their members properly, and being in bed with management. Organizations which have constant fighting between management and the union will in most cases not survive in the future with the intense competition in today's business environment. An adversarial work climate will eventually result in reduced productivity which will cause the organization to become non-competitive. Organizations where there are no unions but have employees arguing and fighting with each other will have a very difficult time surviving. Some managers encourage management members to compete against one another for merit raises and promotions in the organization which really leads to disastrous results in most instances. An environment where managers, supervisors, and employees are free to take risks with the knowledge that they have the support of upper management in a non-competitive environment are the organizations that have the best chance of survival. Some managers truly care about their employees and desire to implement a participative management program to give them a chance to self-actualize and use their full potential on their jobs. A manager's job is to coach and nurture their employees to help them develop their abilities on their jobs. A manager who sincerely cares about his employees in this manner will in most instances be a successful manager in todays' business environment. An organization can only grow with this atmosphere of caring.

Implementation of a participative management program takes anywhere from two to ten years depending on the work climate of the organization. In an adversarial, hostile environment, the first step in an employee involvement program is to have offsite meetings between management members and union officials where they can sit down with each other, have an opportunity to communicate together, and realize that they are not really enemies but that they are all employees of the same organization. Getting to know each other on a more personal basis is definitely important as an ice breaker. In these meetings, trust can begin to be established, depending upon the atmosphere of the work climate. Without trust, there can be no employee involvement program. Top management and union officials must be at these meetings giving their full support. Both sides must be sincere in this approach and have a common desire to work together. Some organizations have labeled these meetings as the beginning of a quality of work life program or organizational development. The important thing here is that both sides begin to share their thoughts on the state of the business. In a non-unionized business, this type of offsite meeting would be an opportunity for management to communicate with its employees away from the business premises. Establishing trust and initiating the necessary culture change in preparation for a participative management program takes time, usually years. It is certainly not advisable to start a program of this nature when employees do not trust each other. It will not work. The employees must be ready to accept such a program even after top management and the union officials are supportive of such a program. Usually distrust occurs in an organization because of the inappropriate method in which management members treat their employees. In some organizations, managers and supervisors are told by upper management not to trust their employees as they are lazy and do not want to work. Once this image is portrayed, employees do not trust management personnel as well as other employees, and in some instances, managers do not trust other managers. Survival of the fittest is at stake. An environment of competition among employees has much to do with creating an atmosphere of distrust. Many times distrust results from competition among employees as to who gets the highest productivity numbers for the day. It may be a case of one employee attempting to outdo another. This entire arena of distrust must be changed before a participative management program can be implemented. How does an organization go about changing this situation of distrust? Management must earn the trust from its employees by being honest and sincere in what they say and do with them. Manipulation is a dirty word. It cannot be used with employees. Honesty is the best policy. When a manager says he is going to do something, it is very important that he follow up and do it. Training managers and supervisors on how to manage in a participative style takes time. These folks can be ruined emotionally if they are not taught and given the proper concepts on how to change their style of management. Management personnel need to be told why the organization is changing to employee involvement programs, where this change will take them, and what the final projected results will be. If this information is not communicated to them, they will resist this type of program to the bitter end because of fear of what is destined for them, such as losing their jobs. Employees must also know where this program will take them and what they can expect as far as rewards are concerned. Remember, this type of program should be voluntary. Employees will resist participating in a program of this nature in many instances if they are forced to do it. The reason for this happening many times is because they do not trust management and are afraid to take risks for fear of retribution. This is why a participative management program cannot be implemented "wholesale" across the entire organization. When employees hate management and mistrust them, why would they want to become involved in decision making to help the organization. Their attitude must change first and trust must be established before employee involvement enters into the picture.

As management and the employees begin communicating and establishing trust among themselves, and adequate training is being provided on the participatory style, management then needs to start asking employees for their opinions relative to their own jobs. As the process of employee involvement evolves, usually the next step is to start employee participation groups which usually center around a particular departmental group. Initially, employees will normally get together once a week for an hour to get to know one another, discuss common problems, and attempt to arrive at some conclusions through group decision-making. In the early stages of group formation, employees start establishing trust with each other and look to the supervisor of the department as a coach and facilitator. It is very important that the group decisions involves all members of the group, and that a group leader be appointed. Employees join the group strictly on a voluntary basis. The group members should have received training in group dynamics, problem solving and decision making. As groups begin to form throughout the organization, consensus decision making will start to occur where all members of the group are to agree on a problem resolution before the decision is implemented. As groups begin to function properly in decision making, ideas and recommendations will come forward and management must then be ready and prepared to implement these ideas whenever feasible. The groups should be results oriented and accountable to the organization. It makes very little sense for groups to get together to talk about the weather. It must be results oriented. The groups meet for a purpose, to make decisions and resolve problems. Once the groups are functioning properly, management's role is more of a coach and facilitator to nurture the group's activities and support their decisions. It is not necessary for employees to make only final decisions but that they become involved in many different stages of the decision-making process. As groups begin to make decisions, this is a very critical step for managers as they are giving up some of their decision making power, and thus it is very important that they be previously trained properly, especially psychologically, to take this step. As these groups continue to proceed on their participative journey, tougher problems will emerge that they will eventually decide to tackle. As this happens, self-managed groups will emerge where they will no longer need supervisors, as the employees will manage the department. This is the ultimate in an employee involvement program, where the employees are so turned on to the new challenges awaiting them, that they run the departmental areas which enables the supervisor to concentrate on strategic planning and other administrative functions. The long range goal of a participative management program is to have all of the employees involved in decision making where they become excited and challenged to help improve organizational effectiveness. When the organization wins, everyone wins. This process can continue on indefinitely, and become a way of working life. Employees take risks and are supported by management. Maintaining the group process and employee involvement over the long term is a formidable challenge. It must be constantly monitored to make sure that the groups are results oriented which will prove to be beneficial to the organization over the long term.

IMPLEMENTATION PROCESS OF PARTICIPATIVE MANAGEMENT
AND EMPLOYEE INVOLVEMENT PROGRAMS

PHASE 1
Offsite Meetings
(Get Employees Together)

PHASE 2
Establish Trust
(Culture Change)

PHASE 3
Formation of Employee
Participation Groups

PHASE 4
Evolution of Shared
Management Groups

PHASE 5
Evolution of Self-
Managed Groups

PHASE 6
Maintain Participative
Management Program

PHASE 1 - OFFSITE MEETINGS

Management, Union officials and employees meet together away from the place of business to talk about the state of the business, common problems and concerns, and get to know each other better on a personal basis. These meetings are ice breakers.

PHASE 2 - ESTABLISH TRUST

Trust must be established between management and union officials, then between management and the employees. This is called a culture change. This phase takes time; in most instances years, in larger organizations of 1,000 employees or more.

PHASE 3 - FORMATION OF EMPLOYEE PARTICIPATION GROUPS

Employees in a departmental group begin meetings to discuss problems relative to their jobs and attempt to resolve the problems in a concensus decision making mode. Supervisor is a member of the group.

PHASE 4 - EVOLUTION OF SHARED MANAGEMENT GROUPS

Employee participation groups evolve into shared management groups where employees start sharing departmental management responsibilities with the supervisor.

PHASE 5 - EVOLUTION OF SELF-MANAGED GROUPS

Shared management groups evolve into self-managed groups where employees manage the department and the supervisior functions as a coach and facilitator to the group. In some instances, the supervisor is reassigned.

PHASE 6 - MAINTAIN PARTICIPATIVE MANAGEMENT PROGRAM

Management must continually monitor the program to make sure it continues to be results-oriented. Program should remain in effect over the long term.

Chapter 6

Sustaining A Participative Management Program

Adopting the team approach in the participative management structure is no small matter. It means wiping out tiers of managers and tearing down bureaucratic barriers between departments. Yet companies are willing to undertake such radical changes to gain workers' knowledge and commitment, along with productivity gains that exceed 30% in some cases, and substantially raise quality (Hoerr, 1989).

The key to future success in relations between unions and management lies in the philosophy of and the commitment to cooperation. A cooperative labor/management stance will lead to improved quality and increased productivity; an adversarial stance will lead only to discord and divisiveness (Dinnocenzo, 1989).

A participative management program will work if it has mutual individual employee participation and cooperation in decision-making, if it is voluntary and self-motivating, and if there is an atmosphere of improved trust and individual commitment, support of top management and the local union. Employees must be motivated and given the opportunity to participate in the search for improved methods of job performance, and this motivation must be maintained over time. From the Hawthorne Studies in the 1930's to the Quality-of-Work-Life programs of the 1970's, it has been shown that improving attitudes and trust between workers and supervisors normally leads to short-run or temporary performance improvements. But maintenance of the changed climate and its organizational benefits has proven to be a more formidable challenge (Roethlisberger, 1941).

If participation in workplace problem solving diffuses across a sufficiently large portion of the workforce, then organizational effectiveness should also improve. High levels of trust, commitment, and participation likely can be maintained over time and across large numbers of workers, however, only if they are reinforced by higher level business and collective bargaining strategies (Kochan, T., Katz, H. & McKersie, R., 1986).

The workplace of the future will require greater emphasis on such key human resources factors as participative management, training programs, and teamwork (Premeaux, Mondy, Bethke, & Comish, 1989).

Employee involvement and participative initiatives are likely to expand considerably over the next several years in United States businesses if they are to remain competitive in the marketplace and survive with the intense overseas challenges awaiting them.

Chapter 7

Benefits Of A Participative
Management Program

1. Involvement of employees in decision making relative to their own job gives them a sense of being needed and a feeling of importance in the organization. This fulfills a need of some employees to be challenged beyond what they are presently accomplishing on their job. According to Maslow's Hierarchy of Human Needs Theory, these employees desire to self-actualize and function at their full potential, which is a higher order need. This theory provides managers with an opportunity to identify and understand employees needs on the job, and make an attempt to fulfill these needs. Once management recognizes employee needs, and gives consideration to them in the actions it takes, and in its efforts to motivate employees, the result should be behavior that is consistent with organizational goals(Burke, D. 1978). The needs of a person change with time, partly

because of the satisfaction of the needs. Needs are the deficiencies that a person experiences at a point in time. Needs are energizers of behavioral responses. The essence of this theory is that when need deficiencies are present, the person is more susceptible to motivational efforts on the part of management. When an employee indicates a need to do more on his job than he is required to do, it is very important for the manager to challenge the employee and attempt to meet that need by giving him more responsibility and opportunities to achieve. The employee will feel better about himself, about the organization, about his job, and the result should be increased job performance and organizational effectiveness.

2. Participation can improve the quality of the decisions being made as there is much more input into the decision making process especially from those employees directly involved in the problems to be resolved. When ideas and recommendations are submitted from those closest to the problem, the chances of successful implementation of these ideas are much greater when they have a hand in the decisions being made.

3. Organizational goals and personal goals can be accomplished to the benefit of all concerned. When employees' goals match up with the organization's goals, organizational effectiveness will improve. It is very important for the manager to be visionary, and share his goals and objectives with the employees. Once the employees understand the manager's goals, they can then rally around him to help implement them in the organization. It is very important for the manager to have the buy-in of the employees, and this happens through proper communication such as state of the business meetings. Without the support of the employees, implementation of the goals will be difficult. Once management receives employee buy-in, the employees will develop a sense of ownership in the business and have a positive impact in the business and the bottom line. Employees must understand what it takes to be successful in a business. They need to identify with the manager's goals and vision, in order to give their support. Employees need to have meaning. They must know where they fit in the organization, and the level of their skills. Management should then nurture and develop these employee skills. Once everyone is supportive of the manager in a team

effort, and their goals match, the organization will be successful. If the manager fails to establish goals and objectives, the employees will lack direction, and a participative management program will become chaotic causing management to lose control of the business.

4. Increased productivity, improved quality, and efficient schedule maintenance will be the results of an effective employee involvement program. Employees will become highly productive with minimum supervision. It is very important that the employees be rewarded for their efforts as organizational performance improves.

Chapter 8

Techniques For Productivity Improvement

It is conceivable for you to have more employees than the competition, yet your company produces less, and for you to have disgruntled, low-output employees even though you pay your employees more than the competition pays theirs. Productivity surveys and case studies indicate that increased worker motivation and satisfaction can increase worker output. Progressive, innovative managers now achieve productivity gains with human resource management techniques that go beyond pay incentives. This chapter discusses how to increase worker output by motivating with quality of work life concepts and by tailoring benefits to meet the needs of employees. Cost: enlightened human resource management probably costs no more than employee turnover (hiring and training new employees), unwarranted pay increases, and low productivity. Benefit: better productivity; loyal, efficient workers; higher quality, work, and increased likelihood of staying in business. The essence of employee motivation and effectiveness is the manner in which they are managed. A direct relationship exists between effective management (i.e., providing a work environment that simultaneously achieves company goals and employees' goals) and modern human resource management. Your management success is judged by your skill and knowledge in recognizing and assessing issues that concern employees and by your ability to resolve these concerns with employee help and satisfaction.

- Do your employees know how you judge and measure their performance?

- Do you provide and encourage individual development with training and educational programs?

- Do you trust your employees and rely upon their knowledge?

- Do you let employees make decisions?

- Do you have timely, accurate, open two-way communication with your employees?

If you answer no to all of these questions, you probably are an unsatisfactory human resource manager and have (or will have) employee-productivity problems. Getting high quality job performance from your employees depends on giving employees opportunities for their personal growth, achievement, responsibility, recognition, and reward. Pay-money-is the primary need and reward. Once the compensation (pay and benefits) is established properly, it is necessary to use other means to further motivate and improve your work force's output. The basis of all job enhancement efforts is your recognition of employees' desire to do good work, to assume responsibility, to achieve, and to succeed. Changes to consider in creating a new quality of work life atmosphere include:

From:
1. Detailed job descriptions with specific tasks and rigid instruction for how to do the work
To:
1. Flexible, diverse work assignment allowing self-regulation, variety, and challenge;

From:
2. Structured chain of command, managers making decisions and supervisors bossing
To:
2. Worker involvement in planning, decision making and operating procedure;

From:

3. Hierarchial channels of communication

To:

3. Direct, fast two-way communications;

From:

4. Limited on-the-job instruction

To:

4. Advanced training, educational and career development opportunities;

From:

5. Job specialization in one task

To:

5. Leeway allowed for every employee to complete many tasks by crossing lines of specialization;

From:

6. Obscure, irregular job evaluations

To:

6. Objective job performance standards with measures fairly administered;

From:

7. Careless or neglected safety and health conditions

To:

7. Clean, safe and healthful working conditions.

The quality of work life technique is to involve your employees by sharing management responsibility and authority with them, the workers who do the job. Compensation costs--salaries, wages, and benefits--are a large and increasing part of operating expenses; yet, productivity can decline among workers who get more pay and benefits. Workers are productive with fair pay tied to performance. Ironically, not all employee motivation and productivity problems are solved by pay raises and promotions. It isn't necessary to make pay adjustments beyond a fair industry-wide (market place) level. The tailoring of benefits to satisfy specific needs is part of the quality of work life technique. It is a way to maximize the amount of labor costs going to the employee and to maximize your return on these costs without increasing across-the-board expenses. By making a special effort to satisfy individual employee needs, you reinforce the motivational value of the flexible benefit.

For example, you can reduce unwanted employee turnover and related recruiting, hiring, and training costs by shifting these costs from developing new employees to keeping experienced employees. You can motivate an employee to increase productivity by providing opportunities for career development (training or schooling). At the same time you have improved the worker's skills and shown recognition of the worker's value and aspirations. Such a benefit is practical because it probably costs no more than worker unrest and diminished productivity, and it is probably less costly than a comparable pay increase.

Age, education, job experience, job fulfillment, marital status, and family size are considerations that determine the utility and attractiveness of a benefit. Different benefits appeal to different people. Everyone's needs are different. A younger employee might be motivated by having use of a company car. An older person may want more status like a title or a professional association membership. The list of possible employees benefits and their applications is nearly unlimited. To get the maximum value, you've got to tailor the benefit to the job and your business requirements and financial capability.

A flexible benefit is two-fold. Not only does the benefit satisfy some employee's specific need but also it communicates your concern to meet these needs, creating the kind of work environment that contributes to increased employee productivity.

You must recognize the productivity problem and the needs of your employees so that you can tailor the benefit to meet the situation. Beyond pay and statutory benefits you should pay benefits that provide the most value to your business.

Chapter 9

Small Business Participative Management

Management knowledge and skills for small and large businesses have never been in greater demand than in today's fast changing world. The ability of small businesses to retain their strategic position in our economy and to compete effectively with larger business firms rests primarily on the shoulders of the owner-managers.

Management consists of all activities undertaken to secure the accomplishment of work through the efforts of other people. Both large and small businesses require good management in order to achieve success. In the typical small business that entails small group effort, the owner-manager provides leadership by directing the activities that are described as participative management.

The participative management style is to share with the small group members the decision making authority. This management style takes into account the needs of individual group members and the contributions to task/work assignment accomplishment they are capable of managing.

The general functions of small business participative management are: planning, organizing, directing, and controlling. Effective performance of these functions calls for the ability to lead and inspire other people.

Planning is the management function of anticipating the future and determining the best course of action to achieve business objectives. A plan, to a small business owner-manager, is an explicit statement of the business's future objectives combined with a step by step description of the actions that will be necessary to reach those objectives. The planning process centers on satisfying the two main requirements of this definition: clear goals and specific actions to meet them.

Steps in Participative Management Planning:

1. Gathering facts and information which have a bearing on the situation.

2. Analysis of what the situation is or what problems are involved.

3. Forecasting what the future developments might be.

4. Setting goals, the benchmarks for achieving objectives.

5. Developing alternative courses of action and selecting those most suitable.

6. Developing a means of evaluating alternatives, your progress, and readjusting your sights as the planning process moves along.

Objectives Should Meet These Tests:

1. They should record the direction the business should take.

2. They should provide guides for goals-results of each unit or person.

3. They should allow appraisal of the results contributed by each unit or person.

4. They should contribute to a successful overall organizational performance.

5. They should indicate the philosophy and image of the organization.

Organizing is the means by which management blends human and material resources through the design of a formal structure of tasks and authority.

Participative Management Organizing Steps:

1. Setting up the business structure.

2. Determining specific work activities to be done.

3. Grouping work activities into logical pattern.

4. Assigning the activities to specific positions and people.

5. Selecting and allocation, and training personnel.

6. Defining lines of activity and authority.

Directing is the accomplishment of organizational objectives by guiding and motivating subordinates. It includes assigning work, explaining procedures, issuing orders, and motivating people.

Participative Management Directing Steps:

1. Assigning duties and responsibilities .

2. Establishing the results to be achieved.

3. Giving the authority necessary.

4. Creating the desire for success.

5. Seeing that the job is done.

Controlling involves the establishment of standards and the appraisal of operating results followed by prompt remedial action when results deviate from the standard. Controlling compares actual results of operations-sales, production output, costs, product quality, and employee performance.

Participative Management Controlling Steps:

1. Keeping business plan on target.

2. Setting business standards.

3. Interpreting business trends-results.

4. Interpreting employee evaluation.

5. Identifying business problems and contributing causes

6. Initiating remedial action to solve these problems.

Small business participative management is the achievement of objective through people using the four basic functions of management. Planning, organizing, directing, and controlling. Planning involves creating blueprints for the future courses of action. Organizing involves grouping work into logical patterns and assigning tasks to specific workers. Directing involves matching performance with organizational goals. Controlling deals with evaluating actual performance to determine whether the organization is accomplishing its objectives.

9

Chapter 10

The Participative Manager
As An Organizer

This is the beginning since it is necessary for the manager to recognize and implement the basic principles of organization before he or she can carry out the other functions of management. Some organization structure exists in all business. Participative management is an extension of the basic line and staff organization structure.

Line organization:

In a line organization each person has one supervisor to whom he or she reports and looks for instructions. Thus, a single specific chain of command exists. All employees are engaged directly in getting out the work assigned. The line organization structure is based on a direct flow of authority from the president/chief executive to subordinates. The organization forms the framework within which all other activities take place. A poor organization causes confusion, waste, and dissatisfaction. A well defined organization structure allows subordinates to do their best work in meeting business goals. A line organization is illustrated in figure 1.

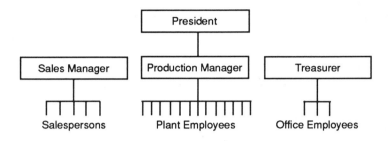

Figure 1 LINE ORGANIZATION

The line organization has a distinct advantage in its simplicity, every employee can understand the organization and know where he or she stands. The direct line relationship also aids faster decision making and makes individuals more accountable for their actions.

A great disadvantage of the line organization is that it is sometimes not capable of handling the complex management and technical needs of a large, modern business. The line and staff organization structure was developed to handle the more complex management duties.

Line-and Staff Organization

As the complexity and size of a business increase, managers usually find it necessary to modify the line organization by adding staff specialists to handle certain specific duties. The strength of the line and staff organization is that unity of command and clearly established responsibility authority are preserved. Examples of staff specialists are human resources manager, a production control technician, a quality control specialist. or an assistant to the president.

Line activities are those that contribute directly to the primary objectives of the business. Typically, these are production and sales activities. Staff activities, on the other hand, are the supporting or helping activities. A line and staff organization is illustrated in figure 2.

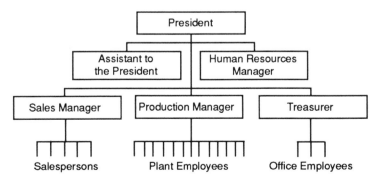

Figure 2 LINE-AND-STAFF ORGANIZATION

The staff specialists perform technical services and provide expert guidance to line managers. Staff managers are expected to make recommendations and to advise line managers. They do not possess the authority to give orders or to compel line managers to take action, although they do have the necessary line authority to supervise their own department. Examples of staff managers in medium and large size organizations include the director of personnel, the advertising manager, legal counsel, and the director of engineering.

Once you have constructed your line and staff organization structure, turn to chapter three and follow the 10 steps to implementing a successful participative management program.

Chapter 11

Management And Planning Aids

Effective Business Communications: Explains the importance of business communications and the valuable role they play in business. MP1 $.50

Problems In Managing A Family-Owned Business: Specific problems exist when attempting to make a family-owned business successful. This publication offers suggestions on how to overcome these difficulties. MP3 $.50

Planning And Goal Setting For Small Business: Learn proven management techniques to help you plan for success. MP6 $.50

Small Business Decision Making: Acquaint yourself with the wealth of information available on management approaches to identify, analyze and solve business problems. MP19 $1.00

Techniques For Problem Solving: Instructs the small business person on the key techniques of problem identification and problem solving.

MP23 $1.00

Techniques For Productivity Improvement: Learn to increase worker output through motivating "quality of work life" concepts and tailoring benefits to meet the needs of your employees.   MP24 $1.00

Checklist For Developing A Training Program: Describes a step-by-step process for setting up an effective employee training program.   PM1 $.50

Employees: How To Find And Pay Them: A business is only as good as the people in it. Learn how to find and hire the right employees.

PM2 $1.00

Managing Employee Benefits: Describes employee benefits as one part of the total compensation package and discusses the proper management of benefits.   PM3 $1.00

Chapter 12

Summary

10 Key Steps For Implementing
A Participative Management Program

Step #1 - Support of Top Management and Union Leadership

Step #2 - Employee Acceptance of the Program

Step #3 - Establish Trust Among Employees

Step #4 - Voluntary Program

Step #5 - Implementation of Program Should be Gradual and not Organization-Wide initially

Step #6 - Intent of Program Should not be To Save the Organization from Destruction.

Step #7 - Results-Oriented

Step #8 - Adequate Employee Training

Step #9 - Take Risks

Step #10 - Employee Involvement in all levels of Decision-Making Process

Chapter 13

Conclusions

Participative management and employee involvement are buzzwords among many business persons and managers today. Many have tried it with some successes and some failures. The benefits are many. The alternatives are few. It means full commitment by managers. It means managerial risk taking. It means sharing decision making which is very difficult for some managers. It means developing trust. It is a new way of managing a business. It is one thing to talk about it, promote it and be excited about it. It is another thing to do it. Many talk about it in theoretical terms. Few experience it in practical terms in the real world.

A manager contemplating a move to participative management must be well aware of the ramifications of such a program. His eyes must be open to such a move. There are no assumptions. It is real life with real people. Commitment is essential. There is no room in such a program for employee manipulation by management. It will not work. Managerial promises must be fulfilled and acted upon. Failure of a participative management program is worse than implementating such a program initially. A confused workforce is chaotic. Lack of managerial direction is suicidal to a business. Changing direction by management in the middle of an employee involvement program which will be detrimental to employees will be fatalistic. Employees today are better educated and much more aware of what is happening at their workplace. Managerial tampering and lack of integrity will destroy this kind of a program in a hurry. Managers must accept the consequences of employee decision making. Sharing decision making does not mean managers are less accountable and responsible. Participative management does not permit managers to lose control of the business. Managers must still manage but only in a different manner. There is no room for managerial inconsistency in such a program. Once a course of action is taken, adequate follow up must be initiated. Everyone must be on board. A program of this nature must be long term to be effective. It must become a way of an employees' working life. It must be a total team effort. It is not a temporary stopgap for immediate problem resolution.

The benefits of such a program are enormous. Developing and using employee skills and ideas is essential. Identifying employees' needs on the job and meeting those needs is critical to business success. Listening to employee recommendations and suggestions makes only good common sense. An organization that has a dedicated, challenged workforce, committed to meeting managerial goals in the most efficient manner, is an organization that will survive in todays highly competitive environment. Survival is at stake in many American businesses today. Those organizations that are sincerely concerned about their employees, treat them with dignity and respect, and involve them in the business operations, have the best chance of survival. The rewards of such a program are enormous. When the business wins, everyone wins. Management and all the employees. It is a win-win situation. The rewards need to be shared equally among all employees in the organization. This will insure continued success of the organization and job security for the employees.

Chapter 14

Closing Comments

The authors have had extensive experience in developing participative management programs in the academic arena at various community colleges and other educational institutions as well as in the practical arena for the U.S. Government, hospitals and health organizations, and various service and industrial organizations. They have been directly involved in participative management programs and understand the necessary ingredients for a program of this nature to be successful. They are not speaking strictly from theoretical terms, but also from the practical real world approach, having experienced actual implemented programs of employee involvement.

Some closing comments from the authors:

1. A participative management program is not a panacea and a cure-all for all of the organization's problems. The purpose for

implementing this type of program is to improve the quality of working life of the employees by involving them in decision making, which hopefully may result in improved performance and organizational effectiveness.

2. It takes anywhere from two to ten years to properly implement a participative management program in an organization. There are different stages that an organization has to go through from the traditional to the participative style of managing. A manager who plunges into a program of this nature without articulating his vision and course of action to the employees will have a very difficult time achieving success in the program. Employees need to know and understand where this program will take them and what the rewards will be. The manager must chart the course, train the other managerial personnel and the employees for such a move. If supervisory positions may be eliminated eventually through self-managed work groups, they need to know where they will be placed in the organization before they will be willing to become involved and participate.

3. Financial resources are required when embarking on a participative management program. The organization must be prepared

financially to implement employee ideas and suggestions wherever feasible, which requires money. It would be very unfortunate to start an employee involvement program and not be able to implement employee recommendations because of lack of finances.

4. A manager contemplating the implementation of a participative management program for his own personal gain to look good on paper at the expense of the employees in the organization will regret this action in the long run. As stated earlier, these programs take time to implement, and short term gains for personal gratification and praise will prove fruitless over time.

It is hoped that this book will help the reader who is contemplating a move to employee involvement to become more aware of the ramifications of such a program, and to become prepared for such a move. If this type of program is started properly, the implementation phase will be much easier, and the long term results could mean the survival of the organization.

APPENDIX A

Pre Employee Participative Management Survey

Please place an "X" in one of the boxes below.

		YES	SOMETIMES	NO
1.	I LIKE MY JOB.	☐	☐	☐
2.	I AM ABLE TO USE MY ABILITIES ON MY JOB.	☐	☐	☐
3.	I ENJOY COMING TO WORK.	☐	☐	☐
4.	I AM FREE TO GIVE MY OPINIONS ON MY JOB.	☐	☐	☐
5.	MY SUPERVISOR LISTENS TO ME.	☐	☐	☐
6.	THE WORK CLIMATE IS NOT ADVERSARIAL IN NATURE.	☐	☐	☐
7.	I AM MOTIVATED TO DO A GOOD JOB.	☐	☐	☐
8.	MY FAMILY IS PROUD OF ME THAT I WORK HERE.	☐	☐	☐
9.	I AM PROUD TO WORK HERE.	☐	☐	☐
10.	I AM PAID WELL TO WORK HERE.	☐	☐	☐
11.	I LIKE MY SUPERVISOR.	☐	☐	☐
12.	MANAGEMENT ENCOURAGES ME TO GIVE MY OPINIONS.	☐	☐	☐
13.	I AM TREATED WITH DIGNITY AND RESPECT ON MY JOB.	☐	☐	☐
14.	I FEEL IMPORTANT ON MY JOB.	☐	☐	☐
15.	I HAVE CONFIDENCE IN MANAGEMENT.	☐	☐	☐

How To Start A Participative Management Program

		YES	SOMETIMES	NO
16.	I AM COMMITTED TO DOING A GOOD JOB.	☐	☐	☐
17.	I HAVE A GOOD RELATIONSHIP WITH MY SUPERVISOR.	☐	☐	☐
18.	I ENJOY MY PHYSICAL WORK ENVIRONMENT.	☐	☐	☐
19.	WE WORK AS A TEAM HERE.	☐	☐	☐
20.	TEAMWORK IS ENCOURAGED HERE.	☐	☐	☐
21.	I AM UTILIZED PROPERLY BY MANAGEMENT.	☐	☐	☐
22.	UNION-MANAGEMENT RELATIONS ARE GOOD HERE.	☐	☐	☐
23.	MANAGEMENT GIVES ME AN OPPORTUNITY FOR SELF DEVELOPMENT ON MY JOB.	☐	☐	☐
24.	MY JOB HAS A POSITIVE IMPACT ON MY PERSONAL LIFE.	☐	☐	☐
25.	I AM RESPECTED BY PEOPLE IN THE COMMUNITY BECAUSE I WORK HERE.	☐	☐	☐
26.	I AM TREATED FAIRLY HERE.	☐	☐	☐
27.	I RESPECT MY SUPERVISOR.	☐	☐	☐
28.	I AM PLEASED WITH THE BENEFITS HERE.	☐	☐	☐
29.	I AM LOYAL TO THIS COMPANY.	☐	☐	☐
30.	EMPLOYEES ARE ADVANCED AND PROMOTED BASED ON MERIT.	☐	☐	☐
31.	I FEEL SECURE IN MY JOB HERE.	☐	☐	☐
32.	I HAVE A GOOD FUTURE WITH THIS COMPANY.	☐	☐	☐
33.	MY JOB IS MEETING MY PERSONAL CAREER GOALS.	☐	☐	☐
34.	THE DEMANDS OF MY JOB ARE REASONABLE ON ME.	☐	☐	☐

Appendix A

	YES	SOMETIMES	NO
35. MY JOB IS NOT STRESSFUL ON ME.	☐	☐	☐
36. I CAN FREELY DISAGREE WITH MY SUPERVISOR.	☐	☐	☐
37. MY JOB IS NOT DEMEANING TO ME.	☐	☐	☐
38. THE COMPANY IS WILLING TO USE MY TALENTS AND ABILITIES.	☐	☐	☐
39. COMMUNICATION IS GOOD HERE.	☐	☐	☐
40. I TRUST MY SUPERVISOR.	☐	☐	☐
41. I TRUST MY FELLOW EMPLOYEES.	☐	☐	☐
42. EMPLOYEES ARE WILLING TO HELP EACH OTHER ON THE JOB.	☐	☐	☐
43. I KNOW WHAT IS HAPPENING IN THIS COMPANY.	☐	☐	☐
44. THIS COMPANY HAS A GOOD FUTURE.	☐	☐	☐
45. MY PERSONAL GOALS LINE UP WITH THE COMPANY GOALS.	☐	☐	☐
46. THIS COMPANY HAS A VISION.	☐	☐	☐
47. I KNOW WHAT THE VISION OF THIS COMPANY IS.	☐	☐	☐
48. THIS COMPANY HAS GOALS AND OBJECTIVES.	☐	☐	☐
49. I KNOW WHAT THE GOALS AND OBJECTIVES ARE OF THIS COMPANY.	☐	☐	☐
50. THIS COMPANY IS WELL MANAGED.	☐	☐	☐

IF MOST OF YOUR CHECKS ARE IN THE FIRST BOX, YOU PROBABLY ARE READY FOR AN EMPLOYEE INVOLVEMENT AND PARTICIPATIVE MANAGEMENT PROGRAM. IF MOST OF YOUR CHECKS ARE IN THE SECOND BOX, SOME CHANGES NEED TO BE MADE IN YOUR WORK ENVIRONMENT BEFORE YOU ARE READY TO BECOME INVOLVED IN A PARTICIPATIVE MANAGEMENT PROGRAM. IF MOST OF YOUR CHECKS ARE IN THE THIRD BOX, YOU ARE NOT READY TO BECOME INVOLVED IN AN EMPLOYEE INVOLVEMENT AND PARTICIPATIVE MANAGEMENT PROGRAM.

APPENDIX B

Post Employee Participative Management Survey

Please place an "X" in one of the boxes below.

		YES	SOMETIMES	NO
1.	I ENJOY PARTICIPATING IN PROBLEM-SOLVING GROUPS.	☐	☐	☐
2.	TEAMWORK IS ENCOURAGED IN THIS COMPANY.	☐	☐	☐
3.	EMPLOYEES ARE WILLING TO HELP EACH OTHER HERE.	☐	☐	☐
4.	MY SUPERVISOR ENCOURAGES EMPLOYEE INVOLVEMENT IN OUR DEPARTMENT.	☐	☐	☐
5.	I AM ASKED FOR MY OPINIONS ON MY JOB.	☐	☐	☐
6.	I ENJOY COMING TO WORK.	☐	☐	☐
7.	I ENJOY BEING A TEAM MEMBER.	☐	☐	☐
8.	THE COMPANY IS CONCERNED ABOUT MY NEEDS ON THE JOB.	☐	☐	☐
9.	I AM BEING CHALLENGED ON MY JOB.	☐	☐	☐
10.	I AM USING MY ABILITIES ON MY JOB.	☐	☐	☐
11.	I FEEL IMPORTANT ON MY JOB.	☐	☐	☐
12.	I AM CONTRIBUTING TO THE FUTURE OF THIS COMPANY.	☐	☐	☐
13.	MY WORK ENVIRONMENT IS ONE OF TRUST AND COOPERATION.	☐	☐	☐
14.	I AM ABLE TO FREELY DISAGREE WITH MY SUPERVISOR.	☐	☐	☐

How To Start A Participative Management Program

		YES	SOMETIMES	NO
15.	I TRUST MY SUPERVISOR.	☐	☐	☐
16.	I TRUST MY FELLOW WORKERS.	☐	☐	☐
17.	I HAVE THE OPPORTUNITY FOR SELF-DEVELOPMENT ON MY JOB.	☐	☐	☐
18.	I AM ABLE TO DISAGREE WITH MY FELLOW WORKERS AND STILL BE ACCEPTED AS A TEAM MEMBER.	☐	☐	☐
19.	I AM MOTIVATED TO DO A GOOD JOB.	☐	☐	☐
20.	I LIKE THE WAY THIS COMPANY TREATS ITS EMPLOYEES.	☐	☐	☐
21.	I UNDERSTAND HOW THIS COMPANY IS DOING FINANCIALLY.	☐	☐	☐
22.	THIS COMPANY IS IMPORTANT TO ME AND MY FAMILY.	☐	☐	☐
23.	MANAGEMENT ENCOURAGES AND NURTURES ME ON MY JOB.	☐	☐	☐
24.	MANAGEMENT HAS DRAWN THE BEST OUT OF ME ON MY JOB.	☐	☐	☐
25.	I PREFER A SELF MANAGED WORK GROUP.	☐	☐	☐
26.	I AM TREATED WITH RESPECT ON MY JOB.	☐	☐	☐
27.	THIS COMPANY REALLY CARES ABOUT ME.	☐	☐	☐
28.	I HAVE CONFIDENCE IN MANAGEMENT.	☐	☐	☐
29.	THIS COMPANY IS CONCERNED ABOUT SHARING ITS REWARDS WITH THE EMPLOYEES.	☐	☐	☐
30.	PARTICIPATIVE MANAGEMENT IS WORKING HERE.	☐	☐	☐
31.	MANAGEMENT SUPPORTS THE DECISIONS THAT I MAKE ON MY JOB.	☐	☐	☐

Appendix B

	YES	SOMETIMES	NO
32. I AM PERMITTED TO TAKE RISKS ON MY JOB.	☐	☐	☐
33. I FEEL A PART OF THIS COMPANY.	☐	☐	☐
34. I AM FREE TO MAKE RECOMMENDATIONS TO TOP MANAGEMENT HERE.	☐	☐	☐
35. I PREFER PARTICIPATIVE MANAGEMENT OVER THE TRADITIONAL MANAGEMENT APPROACH.	☐	☐	☐
36. MANAGEMENT IS CONSIDERATE OF OUR IDEAS.	☐	☐	☐
37. THE COMPANY IS CONCERNED THAT THE EMPLOYEES ARE HAPPY ON THEIR JOB.	☐	☐	☐
38. I PREFER BEING A PART OF THE DECISION MAKING PROCESS.	☐	☐	☐
39. MANAGEMENT IS CONCERNED ABOUT MY JOB SECURITY.	☐	☐	☐
40. TRUST HAS BEEN ESTABLISHED THROUGH EMPLOYEE INVOLVEMENT HERE.	☐	☐	☐
41. EMPLOYEE INVOLVEMENT HAS PROVEN TO BE BENEFICIAL HERE.	☐	☐	☐
42. THE COMPANY FEELS THAT ITS EMPLOYEES ARE THEIR MOST IMPORTANT ASSET.	☐	☐	☐
43. I PREFER WORKING AS A TEAM RATHER THAN INDIVIDUALLY.	☐	☐	☐
44. I AM LOYAL TO THIS COMPANY.	☐	☐	☐
45. THE COMPANY COMMUNICATES WELL WITH THE EMPLOYEES.	☐	☐	☐
46. I KNOW WHAT THE VISION IS OF THIS COMPANY.	☐	☐	☐
47. MANAGEMENT HAS COMMUNICATED ITS GOALS AND OBJECTIVES TO ME.	☐	☐	☐

		YES	SOMETIMES	NO
48.	MANAGEMENT IS WILLING TO OPEN ITS BOOKS TO THE EMPLOYEES.	☐	☐	☐
49.	I RESPECT MANAGEMENT.	☐	☐	☐
50.	THIS COMPANY IS WELL MANAGED.	☐	☐	☐

IF MOST OF YOUR CHECKS ARE IN THE FIRST BOX, YOU ARE BECOMING EFFECTIVELY INVOLVED IN YOUR PARTICIPATIVE MANAGEMENT PROGRAM. IF MOST OF YOUR CHECKS ARE IN THE SECOND BOX, SOME CHANGES NEED TO BE MADE IN YOUR WORK ENVIRONMENT BEFORE YOU CAN BECOME EFFECTIVELY INVOLVED IN PARTICIPATIVE MANAGEMENT. IF MOST OF YOUR CHECKS ARE IN THE THIRD BOX, YOU ARE NOT EXPERIENCING SUCCESS IN YOUR EMPLOYEE INVOLVEMENT AND PARTICIPATIVE MANAGEMENT PROGRAM.

INDEX

BIBLIOGRAPHY

Blinder, A., *Want To Boost Productivity? Try Giving Workers A Say,* Business Week, (April 17, 1989), p. 10.

Bunge, W., *Managing Budgeting For Profit Improvement,* (New York, N.Y.: McGraw Hill Book Co.: 1988), p. 5-8.

Burke, D., *What Managers Do,* Second Edition, (1978), p.56.

Cooke, W., *Improving Productivity And Quality Through Collaboration,* Industrial Relations, vol.2 (Spring 1989), p. 299-319.

Dinnocenzo, D., *Labor/Management Cooperation,* Training & Development Journal, (May 1989), p. 40.

Farish, P., *QWL Report,* Personnel Administrator, (March 1986), p. 18.

Farish, P., *New Work System,* Personnel Administrator, (February 1986), p. 20.

Feuer, D., *Quality Of Worklife: A Cure For All Ills?*, Training, (February 1989), p. 65.

Fulmer, W. & Coleman, J., *Do Quality-Of-Work-Life Programs Violate Section 8 (A) (2)?*, Labor Law Journal, vol.35, (November 1984), p.675-684.

Glaser, E., *State Of The Art Questions About Quality Of Work Life,* Personnel, (May-June), p. 39-40.

Guest, R., *Quality Of Work Life-Learning From Tarrytown,* Harvard Business Review, vol. 57, no.4, (July-August 1979), p. 76-87.

Herman, S., *Participative Management Is A Double-Edged Sword,* Training, vol.26, (January 1989), p. 52-3.

Hoerr, J., *The Payoff From Teamwork,* Business Week, (July 10, 1989), p. 56-62.

Katz, H., Kochan, T. & Gobille, K., *Industrial Relations Performance, Economic Performance, And QWL Programs: An Interplant Analysis,* Industrial And Labor Relations Review, vol. 37, (October 1983), p. 3-17.

Kochan, T., Katz, H. & McKersie, R., *The Transformation Of American Industrial Relations*, (New York, N.Y.: Basic Books, Inc.: 1986), p. 87.

Malthus, G., *Growing Concerns: Run Your Business Or Build An Organization?*, Harvard Business Review, vol.62, no.2, (March-April 1984), p.35.

Moskal, B., *The Sun Also Rises On GM*, Industry Week, (September 1988), p.100-2.

Premeax, S., Mondy, R., Bethke, A. & Comish, R., *Managing Tomorrow's Unionized Workers*, Personnel, vol.66, (July 1989), p.61-4.

Roethlisberger, F., *Management And Morale*, (Cambridge, Mass: Harvard University Press, 1941).

Runcie, J., *By Days I Make Cars*, Harvard Business Review May-June 1980), p.111.

Schermerhord, J., *Management For Productivity*, Copyright 1988: p.429-432.

Spector, B., *Blurring The "Proper Separation: Quality Of Work Life And Contractual Agreements*, Labor Law Journal, vol.37, (December 1986), p.857-62.

St.Cyr, R., *Worker Participation And Quality Of Working Life At The Plant Level: American Experience And The Federal Role,* Labor Law Journal, vol.35, no.9, (September 1984), p.539-46.

Tubbs, S., *A Systems Approach To Small Group Interaction,* Third Edition, 1988, p.133 & 333.

Uzzi, J., *What Is Participation?,* Management World, vol.18, (May-June 1989), p.38-9.

Vroom, V. *Work And Motivation,* (New York: John Wiley And Sons 1964).

A Series Of Articles On The Small Business Institute Program Appears In *The Journal Of Small Business Management,* vol.15 no.2 (April 1987).

U.S. Small Business Administration Management Aid No. 5.009 By John Hanna, APD Entitled *"Techniques for Productivity Improvement"*

ENTREPRENEUR BUSINESS PLANS

A
STEP-BY-STEP GUIDE TO BUSINESS SUCCESS

Each business plan is an easy to read, step-by-step approach to starting and managing your special business.
Cost only $9.95 each.

- The special start-up goals
- The size and scope of the business market
- Site selection
- Equipment & supplies needs
- Licenses and permits
- Advertisement and promotion plans
- Financial plan

LIST OF BUSINESS PLANS

		Check
1.	How To Start and Manage An Apparel Store Business	☐
2.	How To Start and Manage A Word Processing Service Business	☐
3.	How To Start and Manage A Garden Center Business	☐
4.	How To Start and Manage A Hair Styling Shop Business	☐
5.	How To Start and Manage A Bicycle Shop Business	☐
6.	How To Start and Manage A Travel Agency Business	☐
7.	How To Start and Manage An Answering Service Business	☐
8.	How To Start and Manage A Health Spa Business	☐
9.	How To Start and Manage A Restaurant Business	☐
10.	How To Start and Manage A Specialty Food Store Business	☐

11. How To Start and Manage
    A Welding Business ☐

12. How To Start and Manage
    A Day Care Service Business ☐

13. How To Start and Manage
    A Flower and Plant Store Business ☐

14. How To Start and Manage
    A Construction Electrician Business ☐

15. How To Start and Manage
    A Housecleaning Service Business ☐

16. How To Start and Manage
    A Nursing Service Business ☐

17. How To Start and Manage A Bookkeeping
    Service Business ☐

18. How To Start and Manage A Secretarial
    Service Business ☐

TO ORDER

Please Remit To:

LEWIS AND RENN ASSOCIATES
10315 HARMONY DRIVE
INTERLOCHEN, MICHIGAN 49643

Business Guide # _____ Title _____

Business Guide # _____ Title _____

Business Guide _____

Name _____ Plus 4% Sales Tax _____

Address _____ (Michigan Residents)

City _____ U.S. Shipping & Postage _$1.00_

State _____ Zip _____ Total _____